Looking in my Mirror
BACKWARDS

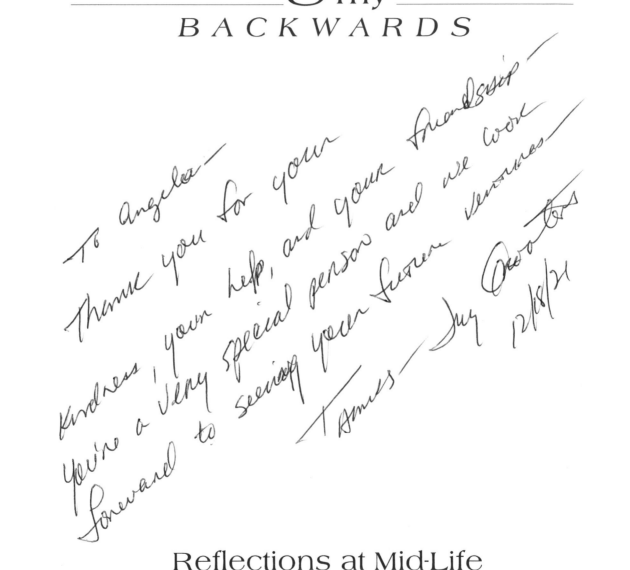

To Angela —
Thank you for your friendship —
Kindness, your help, and your
you're a very special person and we look
forward to seeing your future ventures.
James — Jay Grooters
12/8/21

Reflections at Mid-Life
JAY GROOTERS

© 1994 Jay Grooters

Published by Urban Rancher Publishing
2148 McGraw Ranch Road, DGR
Estes Park, CO 80517 USA

ISBN 0-9641395-0-2
Library of Congress Catalog Number 94-090202

Printed in the United States of America.

First Edition, 1994

Cover and Text Illustrations by Sara Tuttle
Cover and Book Design by LaVonne Kaseman

For information, write to:
Jay Grooters, Business & Living Seminars
2148 McGraw Ranch Road, DGR
Estes Park, CO 80517
Phone: 303/586-5224

Contents

Introduction

————— ℰ —————

This collection of personal poetry reflects one person's journey of self-enlightenment as he moves through Mid-Life. Through the personna of "The Urban Rancher", personal poetry is brought into story form.

My goal is to entertain you, to touch you deep where you live, encourage you to look inward, discover, grow, and express yourself in a way you never have before. The journey of self-discovery and self-expression, once started, is never finished!

Jay Grooters

Jay Grooters

Estes Park, Colorado

Deep within all of us, as we lead our busy city lives, is the urge to get away from it all and return to the mountains, the farms, and the ranches, and lead the life of the Urban Rancher!

The Urban Rancher

It's the dead of winter, and the Urban Rancher
Is getting ready to go do his chores.
'Tis the crack of dawn, and he's rarin' to go,
He's been pacing all over the floors.

Out to the garage, he stokes up his snowblower,
To clear off that three inches of snow.
He knows he has to finish his chores,
Before the cold west winds blow.

He clears off the driveway, then off to the feeders
That he's posted all around the place.
His mini four-wheel drive tractor is loaded up with feed,
He sets off with a grim, determined face.

The first feeder, he loads with sunflower seeds
Especially for the chickadees and blue jays.
The next stop, he loads with wild bird seed,
Which the sparrows and juncos eat always.

Finally, he comes to his pride and joy,
Though at its cost, the budget pinches.
For the Niger thistle is the favorite dessert
Of the pine siskins, and especially the finches.

He'd seen an evening grosbeak among the finches,
It was there once, but hasn't been back.
It must have been the featured professional speaker
At the local Finch Rotary Pack!

He's made his rounds, and filled up the bins,
The good news amongst the critters is spread.
He parks his trusty tractor, and heads back inside,
To his wife, he says "Well, dear, the livestock is fed!"

As he sat rocking on his porch one evening, watching the sunset up the canyon, the Urban Rancher was reflecting on his life, and he thought back to the days of his childhood, and began remembering people and events which shaped him into the person he is now.

In those days, he didn't have a horse — he had a different type of steed . . .

My Bike

As a small boy, I had very few friends,
I knew not how to be someone to like.
So my faithful companion, my comrade-in-arms,
Was my big old balloon-tired bike.

    It wasn't a racer, it had only one speed,
    But it opened up whole worlds to me.
    I'd take off and ride all over the town,
    It relieved the sadness, and just let me be.

On a hot summer day, I'd ride several miles,
Up a long steep hill at the end.
And a wonderful day the top of the hill
At the big swimming pool I would spend.

    It was a huge pool then, hollowed out in the sand,
    Nothing fancy, but lots of water and space.
    There were tales of turtles, and golf balls to find,
    For me, it was a wonderful place.

Thirty-some years later, I drove past our old home,
Up the streets to that pool in the sun.
Now it's much smaller, all concrete and slides,
Much safer, but not nearly so much fun.

    The hill is much shorter, and not nearly as steep,
    The ride back down not so thrillingly fast.
    The trees are much taller, the houses not so big,
    Even the bandstand in the park did not last.

We lived by a park, a block square it was,
My playground for many a day.
The main path which circled it now is no more,
But I hear the echoes of we kids at play.

    A master I was as we played "Kick the Can",
    My boldness and cunning helped me win.
    I'd hide right in the open, and rarely get caught,
    It was the trees and bushes they'd look in.

(continued)

It was a different time then, it was safe to be out,
Spend the evening playing in the park.
We had a few scary times, as all kids do,
But all in all, it was quite a lark.

There was a bandstand then, and every Thursday eve,
The town band would play for so long.
We'd sit on our porch swing, and clap and applaud,
The cars would honk their horns after each song.

The sound of that music on those warm summer nights,
The peace and harmony in my soul.
I realize now are my most treasured memories,
Of those years in my life with no goal.

It's a magical night, as I look back in time,
And the windows to my memories open wide.
For it helps me understand the person I am,
By releasing those memories inside.

It paints me a picture of a peace I'd forgotten,
Of a gentleness of life that's missing today.
As I spend my time working in so many ways,
Not taking nearly enough time to play.

Perhaps one day soon, I'll get a bike again,
A touring cycle, the top of the line.
And I'll take the time to go out into the world,
And experience that feeling so fine.

Of the wind in my hair, of the sound of the bike,
Of the vistas and distance so far,
I'll be out there being in the picture of life,
Not looking through the windows of a car.

I'm a big kid now, so it'll be a big kid's bike,
With all the accessories so great.
For the first time now, I understand the appeal
Of a touring cycle — it's still not too late!

As he thought about his childhood, he realized that in these memories lie the keys to who he is today, and why he does the things he does. So many memories are locked away, with big voids of time which seem to just be blank, but as he delves deeper, the doors begin to open, and he starts to remember what he was like as a child . . .

Childhood's Maze

—————— ℰ ——————

What do you think of, when you look back at life,
Back to the times when we all were kids?
What do you remember of the time you were young,
Before you hit some of life's skids?

    The first memory I can find is elementary school
    As we all showed up the first day.
    I remember the smell of new clothes and blue jeans,
    From the catalogs the clothes found their way.

I was sort of a non-entity then, so quiet and shy,
Fearful of the world and its ways.
I made very few friends, didn't feel I belonged,
My self-worth was so low in those days.

    I remember wishing I could be like some others,
    Outgoing and popular with all.
    Instead, I was a fearful and lonely little boy,
    I was quiet, and skinny, and tall.

My walls were already in place, and I didn't know how
To reach out and be open with friends.
The damage was done to my developing mind,
Not to be undone until thirty-some years ends.

    On through grade school, some talent I showed,
    But belief in myself I had none.
    I floated through life, not even coming close
    To the potential I showed anyone.

In high school I improved, but still terminally shy,
Even skinnier I was as I grew.
I could have been popular, I could have been friends,
But I had to share me in order to know you.

    It was my senior year, to Denver I'd moved,
    Three thousand kids went there, it was new.
    In a way it was scary, in a way it was neat,
    For I could lose myself in the crew.

(continued)

I made a few friends, I was a basketball star,
A good student, not an outstanding one.
But I still had problems letting anyone get close,
If they tried, I'd back off and run.

It's thirty years later, and finally I know
The source of my shyness and fears.
I've delved into myself to understand just why
I failed at relationships over the years.

What about you? Have you looked into yourself,
Into the mirror of those days?
What do you remember about who you were then,
And your existence in childhood's maze?

The Urban Rancher realized that to find some of the answers he sought, he needed to ask questions of those who knew him as a child, and it was in asking his father about how he viewed his son during childhood, that he opened the door to enlightenment about the core problem which, deep down, was at the root of the Urban Rancher's inability to cope with life, and function properly as an individual . . .

It's Almost Too Late

It's almost too late to ask those questions
That have been buried so deep for so long.
He's over eighty years old, with perhaps little time left,
And I almost missed out on his song.

We lead different lives — so different in fact
That there's not been much common thread.
We talk different languages, we go different ways,
But it seems now together we're led.

It's almost too late, for my mother is gone,
The person I was closest to was she.
Just my father is left, and I've awakened in time
To ask him to help me find me.

I delve into my memories, and I find there are voids,
Of great periods of time I don't see.
I've blocked off so much, not remembering at all
Who I was or what it was then to be.

I was only eight then, when one brother fell ill,
Of some mysterious disease of the brain.
He took seven years to die, and the fabric of life
In our family was torn again and again.

A quiet, shy child, I grew up withdrawn
In my own world of fantasy and dreams.
And to shut out the pain, I built up my walls,
Until no one could hear my silent screams.

It's almost too late, but I'm asking him now
To tell me just how he saw me again.
To open the doors, let the memories come in,
And help ease the fears and the pain.

I was lucky enough to have someone to ask,
But don't have much longer to find.
For it's almost too late, and then all that's left
Are those memories locked up in my mind.

As the sunset deepened, and the sky turned a crimson color, the Urban Rancher looked even deeper inward, and almost like a revelation, he realized that in his looking inward, he had finally come to the pivotal event which shaped his childhood, and his future years of adulthood . . .

Little Brother

For thirty-eight years, I've carried the weight
Of the belief that something I'd done,
Had caused the loss of the health and the life
Of my younger brother, of which there was one.

    My older brother and I, chasing each other,
    Running through the house as kids do,
    Knocked him down by mistake, and he injured his head,
    And our carefree kid days were through.

He was five years old then, and over the time,
His body grew up with the years.
But his mind stayed behind, retarded he was,
And that was the start of the fears.

    Very quiet we were, or the convulsions would come,
    He ate with a football helmet on his head.
    And the nights were the worst, for not many slept,
    As he struggled and thrashed in his bed.

I grew quiet and withdrawn, and lived in my world
Of books and fantasy and fear.
On the surface I seemed fine, but inside I hurt,
And I grew shyer and shyer each year.

    Finally he became too much to care for at home,
    And he was placed in Laradon Hall.
    He lived there several years, quite a happy child,
    Until the day my mother got the call.

I still can see her slumped over by the phone,
As she was told that my little brother had died.
The worst thing for her was not getting to say
Good-bye to him, and she cried, and she cried.

    I finally shared this with my father one day
    As I asked about what I was like.
    He said, "Oh, no! Have you been carrying this
    All this time since you were a tyke?"

(continued)

"That's not true at all — that was just a fall,
His problems started six months before!
He'd had unconscious spells before he was hurt,
The disease had already thrown him to the floor!"

Encephalitis it was, the autopsy showed,
Probably from a mosquito's bite.
It caused the retarding, and it burst his heart,
And let him move on to the light.

I was amazed that I felt a great lifting of weight
From my soul as I heard what he said.
The pain and the fear that I'd felt for so long,
Began to lift from my heart and my head.

As an adult, I know it was just fate,
An accident for which there's no real blame.
For that eight year old boy, still inside of me now,
His misconception was his reality all the same.

As I release the pain, and peel away the fears,
I find talents and skills, words and song.
Things I had no idea were there, I almost missed out,
Because I almost waited too long.

*T*he Urban Rancher sat quietly, as the sun set, realizing that he had just experienced a very profound moment in his life, as he defined this key event. As he reflected on the effect that his little brother's illness had on his family, he realized that it was no wonder that he, himself, had grown up so quiet and shy, with little social skills at interacting with his peers.

As he thought about his little brother, he also realized the significance of a certain stuffed dog which was sitting on a shelf in the bedroom . . .

The Floppy-Eared Dog

It sat on the shelf, so used up and worn,
Its fur showing bare in many a spot.
Life'd been a bit rough but it had survived,
Being loved by a little boy a whole lot.

For that little boy, retarded he was,
And needed a friend so very much.
Something to hold on to, to feel he was loved,
That stuffed dog was never far from his touch.

It slept in his bed, got drug all around the house,
Out to play, and got dirty in the sand.
His constant companion, the floppy-eared dog,
Was his best friend in all of the land.

Many years later, the little boy had passed on,
And in the closet of my parents' place,
I found that stuffed dog, all tattered and torn,
Bedraggled and dirty, it wore a sad, worn-out face.

The memories flooded back, the doors opened wide,
So many pictures of my little brother I see
Reflected in the eyes of that floppy-eared dog,
The joys and the sorrows almost overwhelmed me!

Off to the cleaners, I took that old friend
For cleaning and repairs needed so much.
It came back so clean, so happy and worn,
It was again such a great joy to touch.

Where is your old friend from the past
That you held in your childhood days?
Is it sitting on a shelf, just waiting for you
To shift some attention from your busy adult ways?

*I*t was Fall in the mountains, and September is a special time. The aspens are turning colors, and the elk are in their mating season. Suddenly, just up at the top of the hill above his ranch, in full sight, he heard the sound of a big bull elk, bugling in that way that only the elk do.

The sight of that majestic bull elk brought to mind one evening years before, when he heard a strange knocking one winter night . . .

The Elks Convention

It was a cold winter night, we were snug in our bed,
The snow was coming down well.
Then I heard a strange knocking on the side of the house,
I thought, "Great! Prowlers! That's just swell!"

So I armed myself with a huge butcher knife,
And went investigating with some fright.
For the drapes were open, the moonlight was strong,
And it lit up a beautiful sight.

For out on the lawn, all around the house,
Were twelve huge bull elk trying to feed.
Pawing the snow to get at the grass,
So hungry were they in their need.

By the dryer vent, the grass continued to grow,
And their antlers would bang on the house.
I could have reached out and touched them there,
But I watched them, as quiet as a mouse.

I went all through the house, and outside each window,
There was a huge bull elk to see.
I felt like I was in a zoo, but the roles were reversed,
And they were looking in at me!

We watched them for hours, a sight rare to see,
With the snow continuing to fall.
We'll always remember that magical night,
When the Bull Elks Convention came to call!

As that elk bugled again, the Urban Rancher remembered one evening last winter when he was going into town for a meeting, and encountered some elk again — not an uncommon experience in Estes Park in the wintertime . . .

Only In Estes

It's evening in Estes and it's snowing again,
As I head into town, people to meet.
I live five miles out, and often I see
Sights and sounds that are ever so neat.

 I come down the lane and have to slow down,
 There's movement in the fields on both sides.
 I can see elk everywhere as their ghostly shapes move,
 And across the road an occasional one glides.

On down the road, as I approach town,
A big herd of elk is again in my way.
They muddle around, trying to jump the fence,
Caught in my lights, they're nervous and grey.

 On past the bypass, a block from the main street,
 I'm stopped again by a beautiful sight.
 A big lone bull elk saunters out onto the road,
 Showing his 6-point rack in all of his might.

He stands there and poses, silhouetted by the light
Of the town, the snow continues to fall.
A magical sight, then more bull elk come down,
And they stand so majestic and tall.

 By now I'm running late, but I don't really care,
 This is one of the reasons I live here.
 For it's only in Estes in winter you find
 That the wildlife co-exists without fear.

The street lights in town illuminate the snow,
It's a scene for Norman Rockwell, it seems.
For it's a typical night in Estes in winter,
One assumes others see only in their dreams.

*I*t was an uncommonly warm September evening, so the Urban Rancher stayed there in his rocking chair, reflecting on his current life, and the events of the past several years. His Mid-Life had come with a vengeance (he was 45, and although some may think that's a bit late for mid-life, he had a grandfather who remarried at age 92!), and life had been in turmoil for some time.

It had been a time of intense self-introspection, of trying to determine how he had come to this state of crisis in his life, how to deal with it, and what to do with the rest of his life . .

Mid-Life

I was sitting there pondering my life and its ways,
Just thinking of what my life's been about.
Some thoughts struck my mind with power and force,
And my complacency turned into a rout.

    I began wondering: Who am I now, where have I been,
    And where will I go in my life?
    I search for meaning and joy, for purpose and goals,
    For a creative life with less strife.

My mid-life has come and questions are asked,
The answers, some I may never find.
The one thing I know, and won't lose sight of,
Is to nurture and cherish my mind.

    There's a power within me, I've suspected for years,
    But I kept it in check for so long.
    It's come forth and growing in measures so great,
    Impacting other lives like a song!

To move people to tears, of sadness and joy,
To raise them to new unknown heights
Is one of life's greatest joys, to know you've done well,
Awakened the knowledge and lessened the frights.

    I have the power to be a force in the lives
    Of all of the people I greet.
    I may not know the effect that I've had,
    But I make a change in all whom I meet!

The touch of my voice, and the joy I project,
May fill a void in some lonely heart.
Living's not numbers, and ledgers and books —
It's people, especially people, right from the start.

    I am what I am, but what would I be?
    And where do I go from now on?
    How do I find my own power within,
    And say "Mediocrity, forever be gone!"

I have the power to be what I choose,
To impact the people I know.
Just believe in myself, and take that first step,
And watch myself develop and grow!

*D*uring his time of intense crisis, the Urban Rancher needed positive input — a lot of it, and quickly. Perhaps it was part of a master plan, but during this time he attended his first meeting of a group he had heard about, the Colorado Speakers Association, and heard two incredible speakers: Patricia Fripp and Layne Longfellow.

He didn't know that a world like this even existed, and that there were such speakers as this. He went into that meeting as one person, and emerged as another person — his "cosmic flux" had shifted. He also knew that he HAD to go to the National Speakers Association Convention that next summer, and that there was something special waiting there for him . . .

National Speakers Association

"What does NSA mean to you?", he asked me one day
As we sat talking about life and its ways.
"Why did you join?", and "What's its effect?"
"Why do you feel that it pays?"

His questions I pondered and looked into myself,
To see what changes I'd made.
What had I accomplished, what growth have I known,
Has it been worth all the money I've paid?

I was a shy, troubled soul, inner turmoil in force,
In mid-life transition, though I knew it not.
Searching for meaning, for healing and growth,
Positive input I needed, and needed a whole lot!

I heard about NSA and went to the meetings,
And found what I needed so much.
Powerful speakers with powerful messages,
Into my heart and my soul they did touch.

To the NSA Convention I knew I had to go,
Something important was waiting there for me.
I found a new world I had no idea existed,
What I heard there set my inner child free.

The walls tumbled down, the demons I faced,
As I dug for the source of my pains.
It hasn't been easy, and it's not always fun,
But I've posted some incredible gains!

NSA's been important for my growth as a speaker,
As I strive to develop my craft.
But more important has been my personal growth,
As I've delved deep, I've cried and I've laughed.

I'm making new friends, and finding new skills,
As I discover more things about myself.
An unknown voice, a talent for writing,
Feelings and emotions long buried on a shelf.

(continued)

Is it worth the money? It's worth ten times as much!
It's the best investment I've ever made.
The monthly meetings and the convention each year
Are benefits that I just wouldn't trade.

It's an investment of self, of money and time,
But I have to give in order to get.
Give of myself, my feelings and talents,
There's growth to experience, and people to be met.

I took the risk, and went to the convention,
All I had to lose are my fears.
What I experienced just may change my life,
I'll benefit for the rest of my years.

For me, it's been life-changing, and I'm not alone,
Many more have experienced the same.
I'll follow my dreams, and strive for my goals,
After all, life's not an infinite game!

*I*t was there, at his first Convention of the National Speakers Association, that the Urban Rancher heard so many of the wonderful speakers that impacted him so strongly, and as he sat listening, the walls tumbled down and the doors began opening that had been in place for so many years.

John Crudele, Grady Jim Robinson, Rosita Perez, Art Fettig, Patricia Fripp, Layne Longfellow — the list goes on and on, expanding with each year. These motivational speakers gave him the mental tools and courage to look inward, make discoveries, face the demons, and make the decisions that had to be made in order to get himself on the road to recovery as a person...

Speakers

Have you had the experience of hearing a speaker
Who touches your soul to the core,
Whose words open windows locked up in your mind,
Bringing light, understanding, and much more?

      As they speak, you keep feeling overwhelming relief,
      As the pain you've been carrying washes away.
      It's giving your inner child permission to live,
      To love, and to come out and play.

Early in my childhood, some traumatic events
Shut down my normal kid's way.
And I grew into adulthood, too serious and shy,
Not able to enjoy life, to love and to play.

      I didn't know how to just kick up my heels,
      Be loose and relaxed, to just have fun.
      I'd want to, but couldn't, it was foreign to me,
      Too tight a rein had been kept on this one.

It took mid-life for me to open my mind,
Find the keys to unlock the doors.
The cracks in my walls finally started to show,
New worlds have washed onto my shores.

      If I want to change, I look for those speakers
      Who are not speaking on just "How To Do".
      But instead, they help me touch my own inner soul,
      Express my feelings, and find out, "Who are you?"

When I'm ready to change, their messages are there,
It takes finding the speakers to hear.
If I open my heart, my mind and my soul,
The changes come rapidly, without fear.

*I*t was at one of the Denver meetings that the Urban Rancher first encountered Rosita Perez. He was shy, and didn't know what to say to such an accomplished speaker, so he stayed back and listened, and experienced another of those life-changing days. With her songs and guitar, she reached into his soul and opened more doors.

It took more than a year before he could find the words to express his thanks, to send the "flowers" to thank her for her. . .

"Gift from the You·niverse" . . .

Flowers

I sat and listened, with tears in my eyes,
As she sang and strummed her guitar.
"Just sing, said a voice in my heart," she sang,
I thought: Sure, I can't even carry a tune very far!

"Don't die with the music within you," she sang,
As she moved my being to tears.
Her words and song touched the chords of my heart,
In my mind, doors opened that were closed for years.

There's something special within me, I know,
But music, I was quite sure it's not.
I didn't sing well, and I didn't sing loud,
If I had to perform, I'd rather be shot!

Then while taking lessons to protect my speech,
An amazing discovery was made to the core ·
An operatic bass-baritone voice lies inside,
Now called upon, it came to the fore.

The other something special's an ability to write,
I had no idea it was there.
To put thoughts down on paper, to open my mind,
To unlock my emotions and share.

"Send the flowers now, before it's too late,
Don't wait until the funeral day."
She made me realize that for people to know
How I felt, I'd better have my say.

So, before it's too late, I send you these flowers,
Captured in lead and in glass.
A picture of crocuses, crafted by my hands,
For a beautiful person, who has such great class.

Thank you, Rosita Perez . . .

*I*t was after that convention that an amazing thing happened. For over 40 years, the Urban Rancher had never been able to really express his feelings, and over the years, he built up his walls for his protection until they became his jail. After this convention, the walls began to tumble down, and for the first time in his life, he began to express his feelings, and they came out in the form of poetry.

The poetic influence probably came from his mother, who had loved poetry, had memorized a tremendous number of poems, and used to read and recite to her sons to keep them occupied as the family travelled.

So the Urban Rancher began recording his progress in the days following that incredible convention...

Death Of An Old Friend

I witnessed the death of an old friend last week,
That I've known for forty six years.
A person with talent, nice looking and all,
But his life had been ruled by his fears.

He was afraid of life, of responsibility and joy,
And he built up a series of walls.
A prison of his own making these walls became,
From behind which no one heard his calls.

Responsibility? Not for me, he said!
Conflict? I'm not one to fight!
He'd run and he'd hide whenever it got rough,
Like a child afraid of the night.

His self-worth came from others, not himself,
And he was doomed to fail from the start.
They'd play his game, but he'd not tell the rules,
So invariably they just broke his heart.

My old friend, he died — he exists no more,
And his passing was such a relief.
But taking his place is a positive friend,
One filled with love, fun, hope and belief.

As I look in the mirror, I see the ghost
Of that old friend and what he had done.
There I see the new friend, who I want to become,
And I say to myself — "Well done!"

Further introspection revealed a deep imbalance in the Urban Rancher's life, almost bordering on schizophrenia. Changes had to be made, for the breaking point was near, and the positive input came just in time . . .

The Mirror

I looked in the mirror, and didn't like what I saw,
For I was alone, and two faces were staring back.
Now I hadn't been drinking, and I wasn't sick.
Something was wrong, the mirror started to crack.

Was this the source of the turmoil and pain?
Were there two people inside me, in a battle to win?
Which one would triumph, who would I be?
Would I live life with a frown, or with a big grin?

A friend had just said, "It's easy to say no to the bad,
You have to know just who you'd like to be!"
So I had to decide who I wanted to be,
Make the choices, heal the wounds, and become ME!

I'd been filling my mind with trivia and fluff,
My life had become trivial all right.
So I changed the input, began putting good stuff in,
Soon good stuff came out with all of its might.

I've been through lots of changes in a very short time,
As I've made the choices within my head.
An on-going project, the changes never end,
For when the changes do end, it means that I'm dead!

I look in the mirror now, and I like what I see:
One person - healing and growing — a person of worth.
There's just a shadow of the other, and it's fading fast,
Now I see a positive soul attending its own birth.

What do I see when I look in my mirror?
Am I "living my talk" as they say?
If I find that I'm not, I ask myself why,
And start changing and growing that very day!!

As he began to heal and grow, the Urban Rancher realized that there had been a lot of good happenings in his life, too, with many of them taking place right there in the mountains he loved.

They lived on a part of the old guest ranch that his wife's family had owned for years, and as he started remembering, there was a wealth of experiences he had encountered in connection with that ranch . . .

McGraw Ranch

If buildings could speak, what a tale they could tell
Of the life that passed through their doors.
The meals that were served, the horses taken out,
And the thousands of boots on their floors.

The ranch now is closed, only buildings are left,
And the memories that come from the walls.
Of the joys and the tears of the family there,
Through the years the memory calls.

From the roundup in the morning, the trail rides by day,
The cresting of a high mountain pass,
To breakfast rides and steak frys, to songs by the fire,
It was the utmost in life with such class.

The old barn stands silent, it leans to the east,
Looking each year a more unsteady sight.
You can still hear the echoes of horses and hooves,
And dances every Saturday night.

I slept in that barn, when I courted my wife,
A long dusty night at the best.
Seems I slept on a hammer, the horses stamped loud,
And I woke up with a cat on my chest!

The honeymoon cabin sits quiet and empty,
The shingles are starting to go.
But I look in the window and remember the time
Of our honeymoon spent there over twenty years ago.

The lodge stands majestic, but fading in might,
The piano no longer plays loud.
She'd play by the hour, till her shoulders were numb,
Singing songs with an appreciative crowd.

The hospitality was superb, the people were great,
The true Western experience, if you please.
The feelings were unequaled, it's like won't be found,
A place where you could truly "Rough It With Ease"!

Only the buildings remain, the ranch itself lives on
In the hearts and lives of the family and friends.
For it's the people that really make a place,
And the love that they carry to their ends.

Thursdays were special days at McGraw Ranch. It was the cook's day off, so in the morning was the weekly Breakfast Ride. It was about a 30 minute ride by horseback to the cookout site, then a wonderful breakfast there by the stream, and then either ride back to the ranch, or take off on a longer ride for the rest of the day . . .

The Breakfast Ride

———— ❦ ————

A cool Colorado morning, the sky was so clear,
The horses all saddled to go.
The dudes start to gather, the ride's ready to start,
We're just waiting for everyone to show.

    As I sit on my horse, pondering my fate,
    Old Frank's "driving lesson" is quite a show.
    "Rein this way to turn left, that way to turn right,
    And to stop, pull back and say WHOA!"

Then it's up through the ranch, to the meadows above,
We ride single file for a while.
Till finally we stop in a clearing by the stream,
We get off, and my body can once again smile.

    The wranglers take the horses, we saunter on down,
    To where Frank's cooking up breakfast so neat.
    He's in his rancher's outfit, with chaps on his legs,
    To help protect from all the intense heat.

There's coffee and flapjacks, and bacon and eggs,
All sizzling over the wood fire,
He calls out: "Come and get it!", we line up so fast,
A sight that will truly inspire.

    The aspen leaves rustle as we eat by the stream,
    It's a magical morning for all.
    It's Fall in the Rockies, and often you hear
    The sound of the elk bugling call.

We talk and we laugh, and we all know that this
Is a rare experience few people share.
It's not a production, it's the real family life,
Of a ranch family with all of its care.

    For those who were lucky enough to be there,
    As they return to their lives that they've tried,
    They'll remember forever the beauty and peace,
    And the joy of that great Breakfast Ride!

*T*hursday evening was even more of a treat! We'd walk up the meadow to the steak fry grounds, again by the stream. There we'd find the coffee brewing in the huge pot, the beans were cooking, and the corn was simmering. When everyone had arrived, they'd start cooking the tenderloin pieces, and the results were the most tasty meal you could possibly imagine . . .

McGraw Ranch Steak Fry

We start gathering each Thursday afternoon,
For the highlight as each week goes by.
It's something each guest anticipates with pleasure,
The weekly McGraw Ranch Steak Fry!

We wander up the meadow, about a half mile away,
To the area by the stream where we meet.
We hop over the stream, then over to the meadow,
Our taste buds know they're in for a treat!

A huge pot of coffee is brewing over the wood fire,
The food's laid out and ready to go.
Beef tenderloin's been sliced, the beans are cooking,
All the guests have arrived, nobody's slow.

The tenderloin pieces are put into huge pans,
And the heat from the fire is intense.
The cook even wears chaps to protect his legs,
I've done it, and it beats riding fence!

He calls "Come and get it!", we line up with our plates,
And he piles several pieces on our hamburger bun.
Then on to the beans, and then to the corn,
There's beer, pop and coffee, and even watermelon.

I'd put lettuce, tomatoes, and onions of course,
As I build up my sandwich so high.
We'd go back for seconds, and thirds if we could,
It tasted so good — it'd make an angel cry!

We're stuffed to the gills, but we've left some room,
For we know dessert still is to be.
It's Ruth's special McGraw Ranch Chocolate Cake,
The best that you'll ever hope to see!

Then they build a big bonfire, we sit on some logs,
Singing songs, and listening to tales,
Sometimes a cowboy will have his guitar,
And with story and music he regales.

The fire burns low, and the guests start heading back,
Their beds beckon after a wonderful day.
We walk hand-in-hand, there's magic in the air,
Life doesn't get any better than this, I'd say!

*I*t was after one of these steak fry evenings that the Urban Rancher experienced one of those magical evenings which come so rarely. The guests had all departed, and it was just the family left, and an old friend of the family by the name of Edgar Hyatt.

Edgar was one of the few remaining old-timers, an old horse-shoer all bent and battered, with an incredible memory. As we sat by the fire, he began to sing old cowboy songs, and then he shared with us a special poem he had written . . .

The Old Cowboy

It was a magical night, the fire had burned low,
    And the guests had all gone to bed.
There were five of us left — our family of four
    And the battered old cowboy who looked half dead.

His body was bent and misshapen by work,
    By years of shoeing horses, and by falls.
We sat by the campfire, one warm summer night,
    Listening to the wind and the wild coyote calls.

Then Edgar, the old cowboy, started singing his songs,
    In his monotone, gravelly voice so strange,
Not the modern well known ones, but the really old ones
    That they sang years ago on the range.

The wind whistled gently, the aspens leaves rustled,
    And the coyotes howled out their refrain.
At once we were transported sixty years back,
    To when Edgar was a young cowboy again.

After a while he grew quiet, and we savored the sounds
    That we'd heard — a time beautiful and rare.
Then he told us a poem about lion hunting and dogs,
    A personal thing he'd very rarely share.

. . .

He rumbled: "Come all you rough and tough hombres
Draw up your chairs to the fire
And we'll make big talk of lion hunting
To see who rates as the biggest liar."

    "Some folks will tell you that hunting 'em is easy
    To run them and tree'em is a snap
    But pay them not much heed, little brother
    For that is all a big bunch of . . baloney."

"You gotta be tough like the rawhide
And you gotta be rough like a cob.
And if you don't have these qualifications
You had darn well better not start on the Job."

(continued)

"I've run them in snow to my pockets
In weather way down below zero.
And the first fifty years are the roughest
After that you might could be a hero."

"We have run them till darkness o'ertook us
Then make camp on the track for the night
You build a good fire to keep warm by
All you have got to do is wait for day light."

"With nothing to eat, not even a biscuit
Before morning your hunger is acute
And you ask the Good Lord to grant one favor
And that's let me latch on to that brute."

"And along about daylight next morning
After you have shivered the most of the night
You'll make of your mind for darn certain
That a lion hunter is not too darned bright."

"I'll give you the specifications to hunt lions
And to kinda set up front with the experts
It takes lots of guts and determination
And a size one hat and size 44 shirts."

"And whether you hunt them for money or pleasure
You will find lots of sorrows and joys
And if you live up to the specifications
It will darn well sort out the men from the boys."

"You will never hear more blessed music
Than Old Ranger and Spot and Old Red
As they run a hot track down the canyon
With the old cat not too far ahead."

"Now listen to them old hounds a'straining
As each one is trying to stay in the lead
But now they have stopped their running
And I'll bet you the chips they have treed."

(continued)

"Let us get to them, you muscle-brained heroes
Get prepared for a beautiful sight
For the old lion will look down from the tree top
And the old hounds will all want to fight."

"Well the lion has been treed and slaughtered
This brings to an end the wild chase
As night settles in, your work is not ended
For you're ten miles from home in a heck of a place."

"The weather is cold as a well diggers gable end
Things don't look too cheerful and bright
The snow is knee deep and is crusted
I wonder if we will ever get home tonight."

"We stagger in to the home spread about midnight
Both the men and dogs are tired and foot sore
And we tell the whole world to heck with it all
We'll never hunt lions no more."

"Well I've hunted with some darned fine fellows
The most of them True Blue to be sure
But once in a while one can't help but be chicken
And he smells of the fresh chicken manure."

"They tell of a beautiful place called Heaven
Where nothing is known of sorrow or care
But if they don't have snow to track lions
What in heck would I do if I was up there?"

"One night as I sat by the camp fire
I looked at the stars in the sky
And I couldn't help but wonder if ever a lion hunter
Had made it all the way to that sweet bye and bye."

"I am sure not one ever made it
I don't think very many would want to go
But if there was any way of telling
I am sure you would find several down below."

(continued)

"Now kind folks if you have time to read this
I hope you got a big kick from the start
Please overlook part of the mistakes and language
As a lion hunter is not too darned smart."

"There are people who think old hunters live forever
While others think they just wither away
But I am sure they die like other humans
If they don't, why in heck do they smell that way?"

. . .

When the old cowboy finished, we sat there so quiet.
        Knowing this was a treat known by few.
To sit with your folks and hear history made,
        While nature put on quite a show.

The old-timers are gone — one by one they've passed on,
        And with them many stories so great.
If you're lucky enough to hear them tell tales,
        Count your blessings before it's too late.

Edgar Hyatt was his name, a storyteller supreme,
        Take heed, you of a literary bent.
Though he's gone from us now, his experiences live on,
        In the form of his "Lion Hunters's Lament".

It was a magical night . . .

*T*here were also the memories which, in looking back, were quite humorous, but at the time didn't seem to be. The Urban Rancher was a city kid, even though it was a small town, and his few contacts with horses had not been very positive! So, he had no idea of what he was getting into when he agreed to go for a ride . . .

The Mummy

We visited her parents at the home ranch one time,
And she batted her eyes up at me.
"Let's go for a ride, on horses of course,
A small ride, just up on the Mummy."

Now, I was a tenderfoot, I didn't know better,
So I agreed in my innocent ways.
Before that day was over, I'd written it down
As one of my most horrible days.

We started off early, and headed up the meadow,
On up past the Bridal Veil Falls.
We kept on riding and climbing so high,
And we could hear the wild eagle's calls.

And I asked her, "Tell me, dear, just where is
This thing we're riding to, this Mummy?"
She answered, "Oh, that's the big range of mountains
Way up there · that's just where we will be!"

Three hours later, we're at the top of the range,
My tender body is aching and sore.
We stop for lunch, thank God, when it's time to leave,
I don't know if I can stand very much more.

The weather has changed — a storm's moving in,
The electricity's charging all around.
The horses are spooked, it's threatening near by,
It's time to get down to low ground.

A great herd of elk, about four hundred or so,
Move ahead of us down off the top.
The weather's turned bad, we head along back home,
With much speed and with nary a stop.

We're cold and weary as we come up to the ranch,
And I get off to open the gate.
My knees are so sore, I can't get back on my horse,
I'm almost done in, and we're running so late.

I crawled up the stairs, and collapsed on the bed,
And I thought: "This is supposed to be fun?"
Next time I contemplate a "little ride" with my wife,
Just put me out of my misery with a gun!

*T*hat wasn't the only ride the Urban Rancher got to take on that ranch, for there were five daughters in the family, and their father rather enjoyed taking his daughters' admirers out on horseback, to test them and see just what they were made of . . .

The Ride

———— ℰ ————

Take heed, young lovers, and hear what I say,
Before you pursue certain girls with a verve.
If she's a rancher's daughter, you're in for a ride,
To test your courage, your mettle, and your nerve.

    To prove that you're worthy of one of his girls,
    He'll test your skills and your pride,
    As he innocently invites you to join the family
    On horseback — Beware: this is THE RIDE!

Now I was a tenderfoot — the only horses I'd rode
Were under the hood of my car.
I had no desire to climb up on that beast,
But I had to, if I wanted to go far.

    Snip was his name, a big horse was he,
    The tallest one they happened to see.
    With my six foot four frame on this horse you have
    Everyone else a foot shorter than me!

Her dad didn't follow trails, he bushwhacked instead,
And off through the trees he would go.
He'd look back and grin and ask how I was,
On his face, an evil smile would show.

    He'd search out a branch that he'd just barely clear,
    Under which my big horse had to crawl.
    Leaving me to ponder, just how the heck,
    Do I get under that branch at all?

Do I lean back, with my feet up by his ears,
Exposing a rather sensitive place?
Or do I lean forward, duck under that branch,
Skinning my back, and scratching my face?

    The first worked very poorly, although I tried hard,
    At least I did not break the ranks.
    Next I leaned forward and stretched back my legs,
    Not knowing I'd kick old Snip right in the flanks!

(continued)

He was off like a rocket, a streak through the woods,
As I swayed wildly from side to side.
A wild gallop past all, I lost one of the reins,
Both stirrups, and all of my pride!

Hanging on for dear life, I pulled on that rein,
Around in a circle Snip would go.
Up to a rock wall we came, he screeched to a halt,
I dove off and put on quite a show.

Somehow, I survived it, and passed the big test,
One hurdle was cleared, one barrier put aside.
So beware, you suitors of a rancher's daughter,
When her dad says, "Son, let's go for a ride!"

Cowboy country is full of colorful people, with some of them wanting to stand out and be known as "Characters". As the Urban Rancher watched one of these colorful friends over the years, he had seen some patterns developing, and reflected on his observations . . .

The Character

He wanted to be known as a "Character", he said,
There's not many left in these days.
He wanted to be colorful, be memorable in a crowd,
To be known for his unorthodox ways.

    He grew handlebar mustaches, wore a big cowboy hat,
    His language was colorful and loud.
    He drank a lot of Jim Beam, his alter ego came out,
    He definitely stood out in a crowd.

But the outside appearance covered a lot of inside rage,
The unsolved issues were tearing him apart.
He dealt with the surface problems, but failed to find
The deep inner issues which tore at his heart.

    The changing personalities, and the inner rage
    Were driving his loved ones away.
    Unless he resolves his inner disputes,
    He'll end up alone again one day.

He should have been born a hundred years before,
Back in the days of the Old West.
When "Men were Men", and Macho was great,
To be rough as a cob was the best.

    He's getting his wish, a "Character" he is,
    Rough and colorful, he sets a very macho tone.
    But like most "Characters", he's driving everyone away,
    And he'll spend the rest of his days all alone.

*I*n his reflective mood, the Urban Rancher's

thoughts went back to the days when he first met his wife

there at the ranch, and thought about the difference in

their backgrounds and their modes of transportation . . .

Our Steeds

———— ❦ ————

We had separate backgrounds, but had this in common,
We both had our own special steeds.
Hers was her horse, and mine was a sports car,
And both met our own special needs.

My little red car was my best friend back then,
We travelled over many a mile.
It'd purr and it'd talk, as I went through the gears,
It gave me comfort and many a smile.

It was my companion as I searched through the world,
Looking for that special person I sought.
I searched far and wide, but it was when I relaxed,
That I found my special woman, and I was caught.

Her horse took her over the miles of trails,
For it was action that gave her release.
To calm the frustration, to soothe her soul,
She searched also for joy and peace.

She cruised the high country, through meadows so fair,
Over passes so rugged and steep.
Up and down hills, over tops of the mountains,
Down canyons by rivers so deep.

Her father invited me to dinner one time,
Taking pity on a poor Ranger, did he.
I parked my little red steed by the barn that day,
Where her horse was stabled, you see.

As I lounged on the couch in the lodge's main room,
Out from the kitchen, a delightful girl came.
"I suppose you'll be staying for dinner", she complained,
"You're that scruffy Ranger — do you have a name?"

I introduced myself, and she settled down,
We ended up sitting side by side.
All through dinner, we talked, oblivious to all else,
And four years later, she was my bride.

Our steeds are long gone, but she still likes to hike,
Quite often more all over the trails.
We're each others best friend, and life's mighty good,
We've weathered the worst of life's gales.

As he sat there on the porch, the Urban Rancher could look out and see a place near the house, now grown back into its natural state, where they had once tried to do a little "farming" of their own in their younger days . . .

The Garden

The city kid and the rancher's daughter
Made their home in the mountains so high,
Into self-sufficiency they had become,
And decided their own garden they'd try.

It was early July, perhaps a late start,
But they didn't let that slow them down.
They staked out their plot, fertilized the ground,
Bought their seeds from all over town.

The rows sort of wandered all over the place,
(Now you tell us they should have been straight!)
We watered them well, then watched so close,
Expecting instant growth was our biggest trait.

Finally, some greenery started poking up through,
And we laughed and clapped our hands loud.
For we were now farmers, growing our own,
And boy, did we ever feel proud!

The lettuce was growing, the carrots stood tall,
The beets were beginning to show.
By now it's September, and with any luck,
We'll even beat all of that snow.

One fine morning, we gathered our tools,
Ready to harvest our range.
We looked over the railing, down on our garden,
And were greeted by a sight so strange.

Our garden was levelled, mowed down to the ground,
It looked like Watership Downs.
There were a dozen rabbits, just helping themselves,
Munching and jumping around like clowns.

We gave up in laughter, and headed for town,
To stock up at our local grocery store.
We celebrated our folly with Caesar salad and steak,
And vowed to garden no more!

*H*is mind wandered back to the ranch again, and the Urban Rancher could picture the Honeymoon Cabin, where they had spent two weeks for their honeymoon, compliments of her parents . . .

The Honeymoon Night

The wedding was casual, in front of the hearth
At the guest ranch where she'd lived all her life.
A simple affair, just the family it was,
A day of much beauty and no strife.

She'd always wanted to spend her honeymoon
Right there on the ranch as a guest.
To not have to work, to ride and have fun,
To enjoy a vacation at its best.

The wedding was past, the reception was done,
We'd gone for an afternoon hike.
The dinner was over, we returned to our cabin
To see just what married life was like!

We turned on the music and built a big fire,
And we got ready to enjoy the night.
We started disrobing, and what did we find
But a funny and disconcerting sight!

It was tick season in the Rockies, and there it was,
Stuck in her in an inconvenient spot.
But we couldn't remember just which way to twist it,
Do it wrong, and tick fever you've got.

So, back on with her clothes, and down to the lodge,
Back to her mother she went.
For advice and doctoring, she got that for sure,
And much laughter and ribbing was spent.

Soon she was back, all red-faced and shy,
Back to the cabin we'd picked.
We resumed where we'd stopped, and over the years,
Very seldom have we ever been "ticked"!

Not long after the first time he met that rancher's daughter, he again encountered her deep in the backwoods, at the cabin where he was stationed as a back-country ranger . . .

The Perfume

I met her one summer, at their ranch in the mountains,
When her Dad packed me back to my place.
I was a back-country Ranger, a "Smokey" I was,
Patrolling the National Park at a rather slow pace.

I'd been told good things about her from a friend,
Whose advice I valued quite high.
So it was with pleasure, as I looked out my door,
And saw her riding a-horseback, drawing nigh.

It'd been raining all day, I was all snug and warm,
As I watched the riders come near.
They were ten miles from home, and wet to the skin,
They were ready for heat, hot chocolate, and cheer.

I bade them come in, and as I stepped aside,
A strange perfume did I smell.
The smell of wet horse is distinctive at best,
As those of you riders know well.

Her hair was all plastered, she was wet to the bone,
A more bedraggled sight I had never seen.
Add in the perfume, and what do you have,
Is at best, a disguised rodeo queen.

But as she dried off, and warmed up a bit,
She cheered up and talked long with me.
And I remembered what that ranger had said,
There was much more to her than one could see.

Twenty two years later, we're still together,
It's been a good life, all in all, of course.
We still laugh together when we think how we met,
Surrounded by the Fragrance — "Eau de Horse"!

*E*very ranch has its share of pets, and

over the years, one of the favorites at McGraw Ranch was

a big, black labrador by the name of Murphy, who was not

your ordinary ranch dog . . .

Murphy

Murphy was a mimic, he loved to pretend,
A comic at heart was he.
A big rolly-polly dog, a black labrador,
But like other animals he'd much rather be.

The family returned from an outing one day,
From visiting and shopping in town,
There was Murphy, with the horses in the corral,
With one leg up, and his head hanging down.

There'd been bears around, from raiding the trash,
And Murphy watched them for a while.
Next thing they knew, he was rolling his shoulders,
Walking and woofing in exact bear style.

He'd watch the cats try to leap and catch birds,
As they flew across the meadows of hay.
He'd crouch in the fields, leap up at the birds,
And woof: "Go ahead — make my day!"

A rare character was he, a dog full of life,
He'd have made a good mascot for the Dodgers.
Intelligent and wise, loving and warm,
He had the soul of a canine Will Rogers.

Though Murphy's long gone, he'll be remembered
As the dog who thought he could be
Anything he chose, but mostly he was
The best friend those kids'd ever see.

Several weeks ago, The Urban Rancher and his wife, The Rancher's Daughter, drove down the hill to the ranch where she spent so many years. It's owned by the National Park Service now, and their preferred alternative is to remove all the buildings.

But, the Park Service is up against a lot of sentiment to save some of the buildings, to preserve them for future viewing. However, their funds are limited, so it's up to the private sector to come up with a solution . . .

The Last Ranch In The Park

It sits quiet and neglected, abandoned by most,
Awaiting the final decision on its fate.
The pulse of its life just hangs by a thread,
To be saved, it's almost too late.

Windows are broken, the cold air blows through,
The furniture and fixtures are gone.
Shingles are missing, roofs have started to leak,
And weeds have taken over the lawn.

It's the Last Ranch in the Park, one by one they pass on,
Torn down as the Park Service strives
To remove all the inholdings and concessions that once
Brought so much joy to so many lives.

As I wander among the cabins and trees,
I feel just a faint throbbing of its heart.
A remnant only, of that once great, proud Ranch,
So vibrant and strong, so beautiful and smart.

It waits, without defenses, for its projected fate,
With each day, the bulldozer nears.
Were it not the last ranch, its fate would be sealed,
It, too, would disappear along with the years.

But times are changing, consciousness is revived,
An awareness of the loss of our past.
Our heritage is important, but few things are saved,
The defenders have risen at last.

The historical preservationists are rising in force,
There have to be found some ways
To preserve its essence, to stave off the loss,
So future generations can appreciate the past days.

It's a new ball game now, the Park Service is changing,
Enlightened new leadership has come to the fore.
They're willing to listen, to consider alternatives
To the policies that they followed before.

We've made our proposal, a good one, we feel,
That answers the concerns and fears.
If we're successful, the buildings will be saved,
They'll live to see many more years.

As he thought about the families on both sides, the Urban Rancher could see patterns developing. The problems of their parents' generation were repeated in his generation, and it made him wonder about what the next generation would become . . .

Patterns

As I look back at life, I see patterns emerge,
In myself, in family and in friends.
Why do we not see, why do we not learn,
Why do we make the same mistakes with those ends?

I see the pattern of alcoholic uncles and aunts,
Repeated in my generation so clear.
Why don't they remember, why don't they see
What they're doing to themselves, don't they fear?

I'm amazed as a friend from my childhood years,
Speaks of memories she's faced as she's coped.
Of incest and beatings, being used and abused,
And how her life didn't turn out as she hoped.

The traits of the parents show up in the kids,
Getting more pronounced with each year.
If the parents were not balanced, it's no wonder
That the children have a whole lot to fear.

Our patterns assert themselves, we strive to change,
To understand just why we are who we are.
We determine where we are, and what we must do,
To become the people we choose to be so far.

The patterns can be broken, and must be to change,
To be aware of ourselves is a must.
The belief in ourselves, in our talents and skills,
In our basic goodness, and worth, we must trust.

To break out of my patterns, I define who I am,
Where I am, and how I got to this place.
Then decide where I'm going, chart a new path,
And from that path, I never turn my face.

As he sat contemplating the various members of the families, he finally came back to himself, and the Urban Rancher reflected on an experience at the recent National Speakers Association Convention he attended.

All his life, he had never enjoyed the loud music and dancing, and felt there must be something wrong with himself to not be like most of his peers, and not feeling like he fit in with the crowd. Part of it was a life-long low self-esteem, but part of it was just needing to accept who he was, and build on his talents . . .

Being Just Myself

The music was getting too much for my ears.
So I told her to stay, since she loves to dance.
As I left the hall, I felt the familiar melancholy
Settle upon me like it always has before.

I've made lots of changes, there's lots more to do,
To find out why I am the way I am.
What is the rhythm that moves in my soul,
Why don't I enjoy the loud music and dancing?

Perhaps I'm like that Last Cowboy,
Yearning for the open range.
The wide-open space and the quiet of the isolation
Beckons to me, and I'm off - quietly gone.

Like the acorn that can only be an oak tree,
I am me, I can't be someone else.
Just accept that fact and build on my talents
And enjoy life as me, not as someone else.

It's a different music I hear, I feel different ways.
I was asked WHERE I feel what moves me,
In my head, mind, soul, areas of the body,
I feel it all over — everywhere!

It starts at the head, runs clear to the toes,
Down the arms to the fingers' very ends.
A glow and fullness, a feeling of being alive,
That I never feel in the loud music and dance.

I need to accept who I am, and believe in myself,
In my talents and the gifts that I have.
Move on and start speaking, perhaps helping others
Find that expression of themselves that they need.

What am I feeling as I sit here tonight?
Why do I prefer my own company to the loud crowds?
At least, I can hear myself think, and carry on
A nice conversation, even if it's only with myself!

As he moved from his childhood, through the years to his current life, the Urban Rancher realized that time was passing by at an increasing pace with each year. He had just attended his two 30th year high school reunions (he had attended two different schools), and did a presentation of his poetry at each one.

After the presentation, something had changed, for by opening up and sharing himself, he was then able to let people get close to him, and for the first time in 30 years, he felt accepted and felt like he was part of the group . . .

Our Reunion

From points all around, we gather again,
It's been thirty years since we parted ways.
For up to twelve years we knew one other,
Our lives merged for many long days.

What were you like, what have you become?
Are you living life, or storing up broken dreams?
We're no longer immortal, and life's getting strange,
Can you cope with the world's silent screams?

Mid-life has come for all of us now,
The transitions are not often clear.
The questions must be asked: "Where have I been?",
"Where am I going?", "What do I do from here?"

I didn't know you well, those thirty years back,
Because I had already built up my walls.
I didn't know how to reach out and share,
I couldn't love, and you couldn't hear my calls.

Thirty years later, I've broken those walls,
Looked inward and found the source of my fears.
Life is now brighter, it has meaning and joy,
It's still not without its share of tears.

What about you? What travel has your mind
Taken you on over all these years?
Come — open your hearts, share with us your tales,
Perhaps you'll lose some of your fears!

Though we've not seen each other much during the years,
There's a bond we developed back so long.
Like a thread through the years, that connection is there,
And touches our lives like a song.

Take that risk, and come share your self,
Reach out and develop new friends.
It's the second half now, and we really don't know
Just how long it is till our game ends!

As he thought about some of the people he had known in those days, one stood out in his mind. They had dated some, kept in touch for some years, and then lost contact with each other, as so often happens. And he wondered where she was, and what her life was like . . .

Where Are You Now?

— ℭ —

Where are you now in your life, my friend?
Has it turned out like you thought it would be?
What has transpired, who have you become?
Has it been as varied a journey for you, as for me?

　　I knew you back then — thirty years ago it was,
　　In high school, it was our senior year.
　　I was new in your school, a shy person I was,
　　And I approached my new school with some fear.

I remember you well, a gentle person and shy,
Quiet and beautiful you were to be.
Your affection was there, but I could not accept it,
I was afraid to let anyone get close to me.

　　As I look back in my childhood, I see the source
　　Of my fears and my building my walls.
　　To keep people out, to not let myself be hurt,
　　To protect that child from the falls.

We stayed in touch as we went separate ways,
There was so much I just did not see.
You were the visionary, I was the realist,
I couldn't relate to your world, or you to me.

　　You asked me one summer to go travelling with friends
　　On motorcycles all across the land.
　　I turned you down, I was afraid of the closeness,
　　So much I just did not understand.

You tried to teach me to close my eyes,
And smell the lilacs in France.
I tried, but I failed, too literal I was,
I did not believe — I could not take the chance.

　　It's thirty years later, the wall's broken down,
　　I've finally a tale I can tell.
　　Ironically, now I can visualize and see,
　　And the lilacs, I can now definitely smell.

Where are you now, in your life, my friend . . ?

As he stood there on his porch, looking up the canyon at the line of the mountains in the moonlight, the Urban Rancher reflected how the time of our lives seems so fleeting, in comparison to the scope of the development of the earth.

An old family friend, Roy Smith, had just passed away, and with him, the connection to many of the old-timers who preceded him. Those who were fortunate enough to know Edgar Hyatt (the old horseshoer), Leo Baker (goldsmith and peace officer), and Frank McGraw (a real mountain rancher), remember the many experiences and tales about these four great men . . .

The Gentle Man

A tall, quiet man, but quick with a smile,
He'd stayed at their guest ranch for years.
Like the mountains, he seemed like he'd last forever,
Now he's gone, and we're left with our tears.

But there are memories of joy, of laughter and fun,
Of times spent with this person so rare.
The rides in the backcountry, on horses of course,
And the knowledge he was so willing to share.

It didn't matter what side of a topic you held,
He'd take the opposite one just for fun.
For the chance to discuss, to stir up some thoughts,
To see how the arguments would run.

"The Artful Dodger", I called him, I never had seen
Anyone so deft with his heart and his feet.
As an eligible bachelor, there were many attempts
To corral him and get him off the street.

But he would smoothly and politely avoid all the loops,
Without causing damage to anyone's soul.
He never offended, and stayed friends with them all,
And never did any one of them attain their goal.

About himself and his past, he'd say very few words,
But ask him about horses and he'd talk all day.
He loved the Arabians, and had horses in the past,
And stayed knowledgeable about them in every way.

Believe what you may, but I can't help but imagine
The get-togethers in that sweet bye-and-bye,
When Edgar, Frank, Roy and Leo sit around some cloud,
Spinning tales, telling stories that light up the sky.

That isn't thunder, that's Edgar rapping his knuckles
On a thundercloud, reciting his "Lion Hunter's Lament".
And that rain? That's just one of Roy's martinis,
Knocked over as they laugh as the truth's being bent.

(continued)

Frank McGraw

The Aurora Borealis? That's reflecting off all the gold
That Leo liked to wear, loop after loop.
That glow in the morning is from Frank's special smile
As he spins another Muriel McGregor tale for the group.

As we gather together to remember our friend,
To share all the stories and memories that we can,
There's one trait that stands out — we all can agree
That Roy Smith was a wonderful, kind Gentle Man.

Roy Smith

*I*n talking with friends of his own age, and observing others, the Urban Rancher realized that we all have some common issues as we go through the years of our Forties. It's a time of pausing and reflecting, looking at our progress, and charting new courses . . .

The Forties

————— ℰ —————

In our Twenties we marry, start building our lives,
Together, the future seems so bright.
We're attracted by our opposite strengths,
Everything seems to be so very right.

We work hard together, we strive to succeed,
Life's an adventure in all of its ways.
We're young and ambitious, we search out our goals,
There's an unlimited supply of our days.

The years of our Thirties are fruitful for most,
Some raise families, some raise pets, some raise cain.
We rise to success in our business pursuits,
Here on our goals we show the most gain.

With opposite weaknesses we've gone home to live,
The differences show up much more strong.
As time marches on, the intimacy becomes less,
It's more important who's right and who's wrong.

Our Forties arrive, our mid-life is here,
We're at that center point in our life.
It's here that we pause, it's here that we question,
It's often the period of most strife.

We look back where we've been, we look where we are,
And look ahead to where we might go.
Have we been in charge of our lives all along,
Or are we trapped in our patterns so slow?

The kids are raised, like little eaglets they fly,
We push them from the nest to try their wings.
We look at those left, are we still loving and close,
Or are we strangers, enduring whatever life brings?

Does business run our lives, do we struggle to find
The intimacy we assumed would always be there?
Who have we become, and how have we changed,
Is there still a basis for love we can share?

It's a period of conflict, of facing the demons,
We've shoved back for the last twenty years.
It's a time of accounting, the paying of bills,
For the neglect of our inner selves and their fears.

*T*he Forties are also a time of increased awareness of our mortality — we seemed to be immortal when we were younger, but now there's a different pace to life, and more stumbling blocks that we face on our journeys . . .

Mortality

We're in our Forties, and we're feeling quite mortal,
It seemed like life would always be fun.
We've all lost some parents, and even close friends,
And other friends, their race is almost run.

The world gets more crazy, the cancer has spread,
Both in mind and body it seems.
What we're facing in reality is something before
We only had to face in our dreams.

In business it's "Take what you can and run",
Never mind the ethics and the cost.
Across the nation, greed runs rampant,
So many models of trust and integrity we've lost.

Cities become war zones as gangs take hold,
The innocence of earlier days is no more.
The violence escalates, the kids carry guns,
Driving in the big city's now a dangerous chore.

We look around as cancer's taking the lives
Of several dozen family and close friends.
And we're entering that period of life,
Where feeling mortal just never seems to end.

So how do we cope? We continue to live!
Live life fully, with joy and with love.
Find good in each person, each day, and each self,
Find peace amongst the "Push and the Shove".

I control my own life, I choose my own way,
I can live life, or die living each day.
It's all up to me, I make my own choice,
In all that I do and I say!

*I*f he had to pick one common recurring theme in the lives of himself and his peers, it would be Co-Dependency. As friends at the reunions came up after the presentations, it became obvious to all of us that this is not just a new "buzz-word", but a very definite condition for us to deal with, or it will be passed to the next generation . . .

Co-Dependents

We search for approval, for love and for warmth,
From all the people we encounter in our life.
The validation for our being as a person we seek,
Always from others, we look to in our strife.

We're co-dependent, we've relegated responsibility
For our own happiness, we're not to blame.
If we're not happy, it's their fault, not ours,
But we do get to suffer, just the same.

It's only when we realize that we are in charge
Of ourselves, our happiness and joy.
That we cannot let others be masters of our fate,
If we're not, we're just someone else's toy.

I sit down with friends, and we open our hearts,
And compare notes from those days long ago.
We find similar problems and similar fears,
Unresolved conflicts, so much we did not know.

The wounds run silent, and the wounds run deep,
Long they've lain, hidden away, needing to heal.
As we bring them to light, expose them to air,
The cleansing and healing we can feel.

Our Forties is a time of reflection and growth,
Of taking time for the child deep within,
For if I don't face it now, I'll pass it along,
My co-dependency lives on, just like I've been.

*I*t was a strong night for memories, and he

thought about his poem he closed his reunion

presentations with, as he tried to share with his friends his

new-found awareness of life, and to encourage them to

live their lives fully, to go out and create more of those

precious memories . . .

Make Some Memories

As you gather together in our reunion tonight,
And you dance and mingle, talk and sing.
Open up your hearts, reach out your arms,
You never know what it might bring.

We've all changed a lot from who we were then,
The years have taken their toll.
Our weight has changed, our hair has thinned down,
But our beings are now much more whole.

There's not a one of us who has not felt
The loss of family or friends.
The prices we pay for the love that we know,
Are the losses we suffer at the ends.

But there is a balance in life, you will find,
There's a new beginning for each end.
Life goes on, and love spreads anew,
You rebuild, your soul starts to mend.

Reach out and share, invite someone in —
Into your life and your ways.
The second half of your life's being played,
And who knows for how many days?

There's no limit on players, it's an infinite court,
It's up to you just how well you play.
Do you sit on the sidelines and hope some one asks,
Or do you go on out and make your own way?

A reunion can be such a magical time,
One of renewing old friendships long past.
Of making new friends, of sharing yourself,
Creating memories that will linger and last.

May magic touch your heart, may it reach to your soul,
May this weekend bring changes profound.
As you open your heart, your soul and your mind,
You'll find whole new worlds without bound.

(continued)

There are talents within you, perhaps you're not aware,
There is music, there are words, there is song.
All you need are encouraging words,
They'll flow forth, and you'll feel, "I belong!"

Ask permission to hug, don't be afraid to share,
Mortality creeps up on us on all sides.
For if you've lived, you've a story to tell,
You may have your own "Prince of Tides."

Go ahead, make some memories . . ! ! !

*T*he Urban Rancher leaned back, looked up at the stars that seemed to be reflecting in the sky, and thought about what he would say, on this night of reflections, to all those in his past that he had caused some pain.

He had dug down and found the source of his conflict and pain within himself, which had caused him to fail in so many relationships over the years . . .

Reflections

It's a night of reflections, as I look at my life,
As I sum up my life up to now.
There's been joy and sorrow, and the effects of both
Can be seen in the creases of my brow.

Thank you for the joy, for the things I've learned,
During the time of my life spent with you.
We had a lot of good times, of sharing and joy,
And we had our share of the bad times, too.

I really regret the pain that I caused,
The inevitable result of my deep inner strife.
I only can hope that with that influence removed,
The joy will return to your life.

As I look back at my self, I'm amazed that I coped,
And functioned as well as I did.
The fear and the conflict were tearing me apart,
But for so long, I kept it very well hid.

In my forties, it surfaced, as it had to some day,
My demons I had to face the best I could.
The fall-out for you seemed to be lots of pain,
At least the crisis had come, as it should.

As we both heal, and go on with our lives,
I hope you're dealing with all of your fears.
As you come to terms with your own child inside,
Release your joy, find your peace through the years.

As he thought about all the joys in his life, the Urban Rancher also realized that inevitably, there must be separations of all types — friendships fading, divorces, deaths, relationships that didn't work out, and more.

They had just spent several days going to funerals of friends or family, and again the sense of mortality was strongly felt.

One service in particular was extremely moving . . .

Henri

— 🦢 —

I didn't know Henri very well, it seemed,
I'd only been around him in a crowd.
My impressions were few, a crusty old guy,
Rather opinionated, with a life force a bit loud.

    I sat at his funeral and experienced something rare,
    As they spoke of their lives with this man.
    They painted a picture of many sides I didn't know,
    I'd seen only a minute part of his plan.

They spoke of his laughter, of his love for life,
For his work and his family and friends.
Of the scope of his impact, the lives that he touched,
The list seemed to go on without ends.

    His son shared a story his dad read to him a lot,
    As a child, it was his favorite tale.
    About a man and his steam shovel, and what they did,
    What they accomplished — this he did regale.

But he turned the tale into an analogy of life,
And Henri became the steam shovel for you.
He dug and he built the four corners of his life,
They were so straight, so neat, and so true.

    In a few short words, he painted the picture
    Of a man with such a great heart.
    He had his failings, like all of us do,
    My loss is not knowing him from the start.

Henri was quite a man . . .

As he reflected on some of the people in his past, he remembered an old man he met sitting on a pier in Cannery Row in Monterey, California, and pondered on how that old man's life had not turned out like he thought it would be . . .

The Old Man

———— *C* ————

I was walking the pier in Cannery Row one day,
Just enjoying the ocean and its ways,
When I encountered a grizzled and worn-out old man,
And experienced one of those memorable days.

We sat on that pier and dangled our legs
Over the edge, there by the sea.
After a while, he started to talk,
And opened his heart and his mind to me.

He wasn't always like this, with nothing to show,
Just living wherever he can.
He was young once, and time seemed forever,
And he never felt the need to plan.

He felt immortal, and lived for each day,
Making good money, living high on the hog.
He looked back at those years, at what he achieved,
Now his memory seems shrouded in fog.

He once had his own business, a good one it was,
But he never found money to save.
He brought a lot in, and it all went back out,
Like the tide, life took what it gave.

As he grew older, he thought that he'd start
Thinking about his later years yet to come.
He never imagined that he'd end up like this,
A broken-down, penniless bum.

Nobody ever told him to watch out for himself,
They figured he was smart enough to know
That it was himself he had to depend on to make sure
He'd be solvent, with something to show.

The course of his future, he never took time
To plot out and follow a plan.
He lived for each day, and said "Maybe tomorrow
I'll think about that, if I can."

(continued)

On through his life, he worked very hard,
But never did he ever find the time
To put some aside, to pay himself first.
What he's done to himself is a crime.

Business turned bad, his life fell apart,
And now it's too late for much gain.
For what he has left are his memories of life,
I hope they're good, for now he's in pain.

He finally grew quiet and talked to me no more,
Just sat and stared out over the sea.
I tucked some bills in his pocket, gave him a hug,
And went off by myself to be.

I thought about my life and its patterns so far,
I'd finally started planning and putting aside.
It wasn't until my Mid-life I started to save,
But now I'm hitting my stride.

The evening was deepening, the chill was finally beginning to set in, and the Urban Rancher was beginning to fade. So, yawning and stretching, he got up, walked around the porch, savoring the last sights of the evening, the smells and sounds of the mountains, and thought of what he would say to someone who had asked him why he preferred mountain life to city life . . .

The High Country

Have you ever stood by a high country meadow,
As the aspen leaves rustle in the breeze,
Watched the elk browse and heard the birds sing,
Absorbed by the colors of the trees?

Do you remember the smell of the pines,
As you breathe in that clean mountain air?
Have you stood by a lake, with reflections so clear,
Did you ever see a sight quite so fair?

Have you enjoyed the freedom of walking the mountains,
And hiking with family or friends?
Have you basked in the sun during a nap after lunch,
And felt the tranquility that just never ends?

Have you found yourself high up on top of the ridges,
Viewing the vast panoramas unfolding all around?
It's God's country out here, it's all here to share
With you, from the sky to the ground.

Feel the true freedom, the excitement of the unknown,
Much like being an eagle in flight.
Listening sharpens, and you'll hear nature whisper,
As your special days turn into night.

Come join us in our travels, over miles of trails,
Be uplifted, and invigorated so strong.
You'll be overwhelmed by the beauty you feel,
And you'll just have to break out in a song!

As he thought about all the help and support they had received from friends and family during their difficult times, the Urban Rancher could look out and see where they could return some of that support to their friends in their time of need . . .

How Can We Help?

How can we help you, our friend,
As you experience your changes?
We watch you struggle as you cope,
Trying to hold your marriage together.

Your personality differences are really apparent,
The strengths have become weaknesses, it seems.
One's getting stronger, the other's set in their ways,
The grounds for compromise seem slim.

How much of yourself do you have to give up,
To be loved by another person?
In order to reach your goals,
What price will you have to pay?

For every Yes, there's a No —
There's a price to pay for everything we do.
But for every ending, there's a new beginning,
If you can't work it out, there's new worlds to find.

There's a lot of people out there,
Looking for what you have to offer.
Your joy of life, your love of adventure,
Your smile and warm heart.

We've survived our transitions,
And we're healthy and growing.
We're your good friends, and we're standing by,
Ready to help, however we can.

*I*n a time of aloneness, sometimes it's nice to have a stuffed bear to hold at night, when the darkness seems to close in on a person. We were looking in a toy store for just such a bear, when we saw a magical grey and brown bear in the bargain section.

He needed a bit of stitching, so we took him home, stitched him up, and tied a special ribbon around his neck, and gave him to our friend, who was away from home attending flight school for her pilot's training . . .

Sky Bear

He never dreamed, as he sat on the shelf
In that toy store where he was found,
That he would be so lucky to go to a place
Where love falls on such fertile ground.

He sat on that shelf, just needing a friend
To hold him and love him so much.
For he comes alive, and spreads comfort and joy,
When warmed by your special touch.

In good times and bad, in sadness and joy,
Or if you feel all afraid and alone,
Just reach out for him, and give him a hug,
And your fears will soon be all gone!

For he's a SKY BEAR — he'll bring you home safe
From your journeys all over the sky.
He'll watch over you as you hike through the woods,
And on any strange venture you try!

He's a SKY BEAR — he gives your dreams wings,
Because all the power is within you
To accomplish your goals, in spite of the odds,
To reach High, live Heroic, and True!

Your SKY BEAR looks up with his heart and his soul
To reach out, to comfort and love.
And no matter what comes, he'll always be there,
To brighten your life like a light from above!

*T*he Urban Rancher has been in the lodging business in Estes Park for close to 20 years, and as he shifted his reflections from their friends to some of the experiences at work, he realized that there had been some really humorous things over the years.

It also seemed like the major breakdowns didn't happen until he went away for the convention in July each summer . . .

Just One Of Those Days

I called from the convention to see how she was,
To see how the days had gone by.
For we run a motel in the Colorado mountains,
And I'm off conventioning in the month of July.

Now in the lodging business this is the time
We're the busiest we can possibly be.
For me to be gone is really a strain,
Something always happens, and it's never to me.

She answered the phone, I could tell by her voice,
By the strain and the pain in each phrase,
That it hadn't gone smooth, and hadn't gone well,
She'd not had the very best of days.

There'd been a huge storm, the waters rushed in,
Flooding the pump house and three rooms beside.
With no water pressure for most of the place,
I'd have understood if she'd sat down and cried!

The lightning struck close, electricity went out,
There was no TV, no phone, and no light.
Some one fell in a bathroom, a towel got flushed,
And plugged up the sewer so tight.

There were drunks in the pool, making noise galore,
Upset guests coming the next morning to complain.
The handyman drilled through a live electrical wire,
Sparks were flying through the office again.

It was pouring down rain at seven at night,
A backhoe was digging holes in the lot.
Trying to find the sewer line to fix,
If she'd had a gun, herself she'd have shot!

So I asked her so quietly, just how are things?
How's everything, are there any bright rays?
And she replied calmly, with that "Innkeeper's Shrug",
"Not much unusual, it's just one of those days!"

113

*S*ome mornings, as they get the morning chores done in the motel office before opening up for the day, the Urban Rancher can look out and see people circling the parking lot, waiting for the door to open, and his off-beat mind conjured up a vision of the vultures circling in the western sky, waiting for the kill . . .

The Vultures

———— ℭ ————

The sky's getting lighter, they start to appear,
As the darkness begins to wane.
They wait for their quarry, testing the air,
They know they're not waiting in vain.

We see them outside, circling the lot,
Waiting for the opening door.
The coffee vultures are gathering now,
They smell the coffee's particular odor.

We open the door, and quickly step back,
To avoid being run down apace.
They stream into the office, one thought in mind,
"COFFEE! And don't look into my face!"

Watch out! There's one in curlers,
Complete with bathrobe and scowl.
There's a big grouchy bear, rumpled and bleary,
They're funny enough to just make you howl!

Some come marching in with grim, silent faces,
Looking only at the floor as they walk.
Acknowledging no greeting, only coffee they want,
The last thing they want is to talk!

Then there's the more greedy of the vultures,
Who innocently smile as they load
Bunches of packets of hot chocolate and tea,
And creamers, "Just for the road!"

There are some nice vultures, give them their due,
They're smiling and cheerful as they arrive.
They're vibrant and positive, a joy to behold,
Not like those who look more dead than alive.

We hustle around for several hours, it seems,
Making pot after pot as they drink.
When finally sated, they quietly depart,
Back to their perches, to ponder and think.

As he comes to the end of his day of reflecting, of looking into the mirror of his life, he looked up at the stars and smiled, remembering the Little Prince and his flower, and felt some of the inner peace that he had been looking for beginning to take shape in his soul . . .

Looking In My Mirror Backwards

———— ℰ ————

As I come to the end of this day of reflections,
Of looking back at my life from its start,
I look at that person I see in my mirror,
And see that I've not always been smart.

But I haven't done badly when I total the score,
As I see the changes that are mine.
It would have been better to become more aware
Much earlier in life, but that's just fine.

It's never too late to start looking for change,
To improve on the person you were.
Whether you're twenty or forty, or sixty and more,
You're in charge of your life, that's for sure.

We live in a country of opportunity unbounded,
And we have the privilege of having the space
To not just survive, but look into ourselves,
And examine the issues we face.

The world's getting crazier, the violence escalates,
As it creeps into the fabric of our life.
It's up to us to retain our perspective and balance,
To find the inner peace among the daily strife.

As I look in my mirror backwards, what will I see,
And what will I do to change my ways?
Now that I've looked backwards, it's forward I go,
Charting a new course for my days.

The road I've chosen won't always be smooth,
And there will always be obstacles to find.
I may stumble and fall, but I'll always get up,
And go on with this incredible journey of the mind.

And where are you in your journey, my friend?
Are you waiting to start, or are you on your way?
Look in your mirror backwards, it's not hard to do,
And you'll start going forwards each day.

Go ahead, take that big step onto the road of life —
You never know where it will take you.
For to grow and to change, to heal and improve,
The reflections from your mirror will ring true.

And then he went inside and went to bed, looking forward to another day in the life of the Urban Rancher . . . . . .

ORDER FORM

TELEPHONE ORDERS: Call 303-586-5224.
Have your VISA or MASTERCARD ready.

FAX ORDERS: 303-586-6249

POSTAL ORDERS: Urban Rancher Publishing
attn: Jay Grooters
2148 McGraw Ranch Rd, DGR
Estes Park, CO 80517 USA

Please send the following books. I understand that I may return any books for a full refund -- for any reason, no questions asked.

Looking In My Mirror Backwards

PRICE OF BOOK: $13.95 U.S. Funds x _____ (no. of copies) = $ _____

SALES TAX: Please add 3% for books shipped to Colorado addresses $ _____

SHIPPING: **Book Rate**: $2.00 for 1st book and $.75 for each additional book $ _____
(Surface shipping may take three to four weeks)
Air Mail: $3.50 per book (sent Post Office 2nd Day Delivery) $ _____

TOTAL DUE $ _____

PAYMENT: ❑ Check Enclosed
❑ VISA   ❑ MASTERCARD

Card Number_____-_____-_____-_____ Exp. Date: _____/ _____

Name on card _____

Signature _____

SHIP TO: Name (please print) _____

Mailing Address _____

City _____ State _____ Zip _____

Phone: Day (_____) _____ Evening (_____) _____